FINGERPICKING Lullabyes

Arrangements by Chad Johnson

ISBN 978-1-4234-8742-5

HAL•LEONARD®
CORPORATION

7777 W. BLUEMOUND RD. P.O. BOX 13819 MILWAUKEE, WI 53213

Visit Hal Leonard Online at
www.halleonard.com

INTRODUCTION TO FINGERSTYLE GUITAR

Fingerstyle (a.k.a. fingerpicking) is a guitar technique that means you literally pick the strings with your right-hand fingers and thumb. This contrasts with the conventional technique of strumming and playing single notes with a pick (a.k.a. flatpicking). For fingerpicking, you can use any type of guitar: acoustic steel-string, nylon-string classical, or electric.

THE RIGHT HAND

The most common right-hand position is shown here.

Use a high wrist; arch your palm as if you were holding a ping-pong ball. Keep the thumb outside and away from the fingers, and let the fingers do the work rather than lifting your whole hand.

The thumb generally plucks the bottom strings with downstrokes on the left side of the thumb and thumbnail. The other fingers pluck the higher strings using upstrokes with the fleshy tip of the fingers and fingernails. The thumb and fingers should pluck one string per stroke and not brush over several strings.

Another picking option you may choose to use is called hybrid picking (a.k.a. plectrum-style fingerpicking). Here, the pick is usually held between the thumb and first finger, and the three remaining fingers are assigned to pluck the higher strings.

THE LEFT HAND

The left-hand fingers are numbered 1 through 4.

Be sure to keep your fingers arched, with each joint bent; if they flatten out across the strings, they will deaden the sound when you fingerpick. As a general rule, let the strings ring as long as possible when playing fingerstyle.

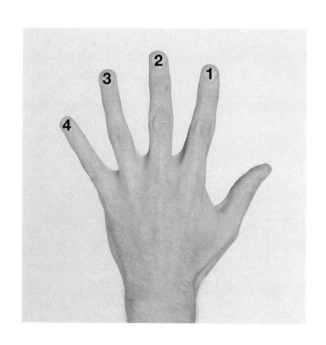

Appalachian Lullaby

Words and Music by Tanya Goodman and Michael Sykes

Intro
Moderately fast

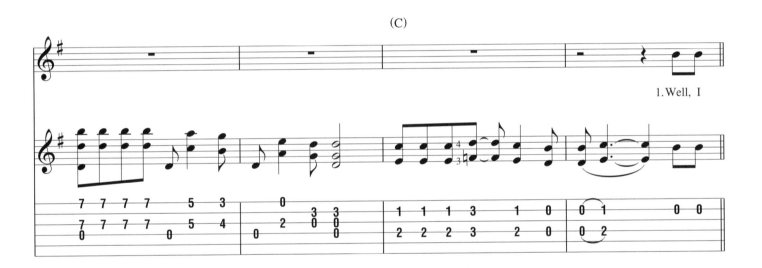

1. Well, I

Verse

love my __ ba - by, sweet and fair. __ You've got the sky in your eyes, the sun in your __ hair. I
ba - by __ you'll be sleep - ing soon, __ kissed by the gold - en stars and __ moon.

Sleep — my ba - by, nes - tled in your mam - ma's arms. —

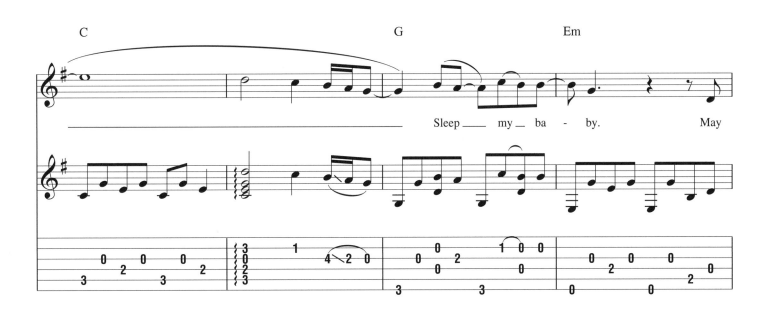

Sleep — my ba - by. May

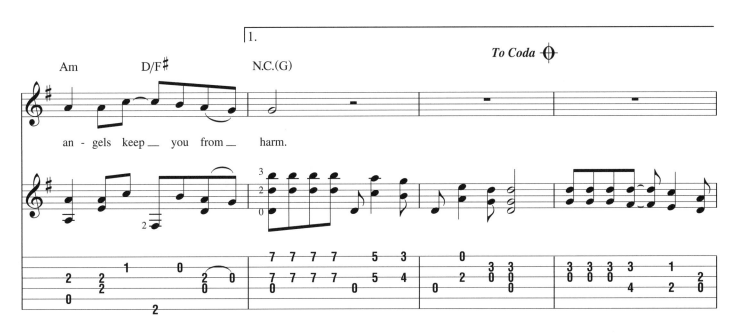

an - gels keep — you from — harm.

Bella's Lullaby

from the Summit Entertainment film TWILIGHT
Composed by Carter Burwell

Drop D tuning:
(low to high) D-A-D-G-B-E

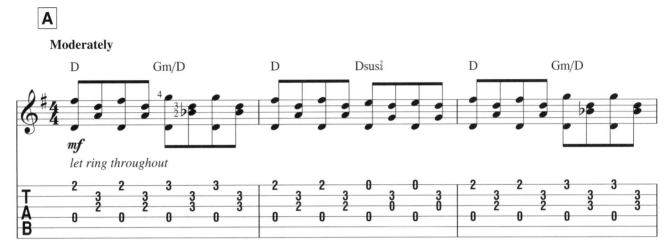

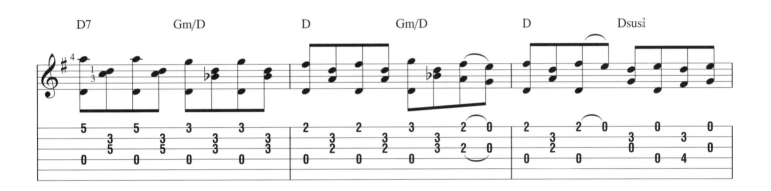

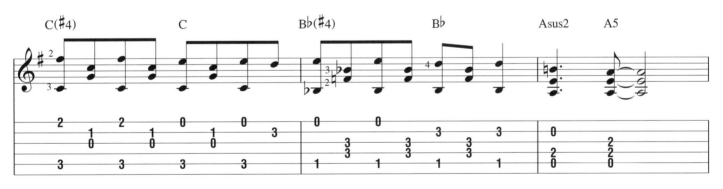

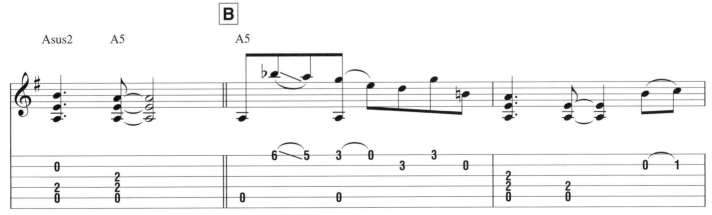

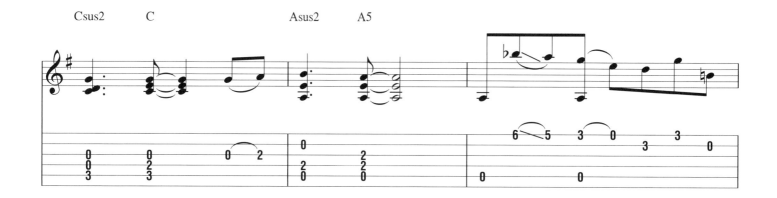

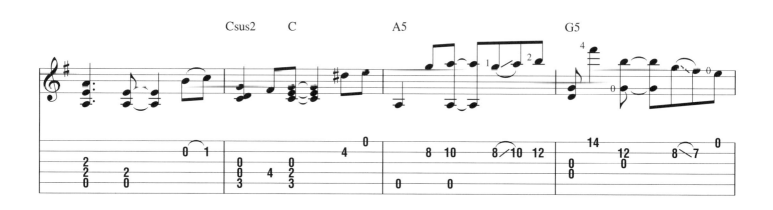

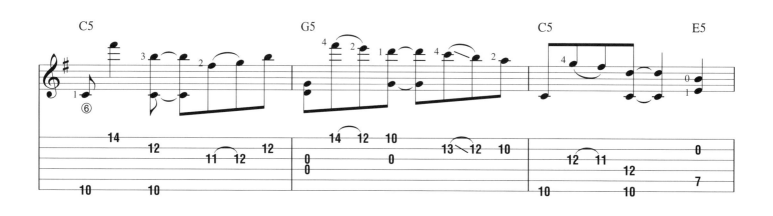

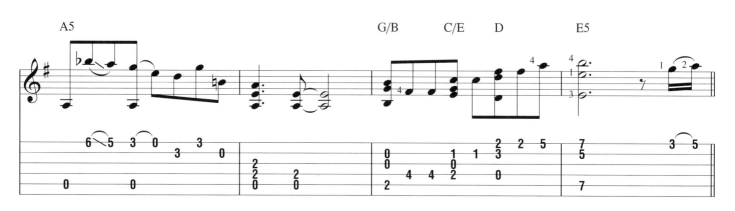

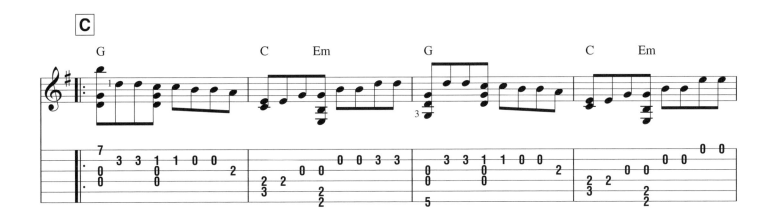

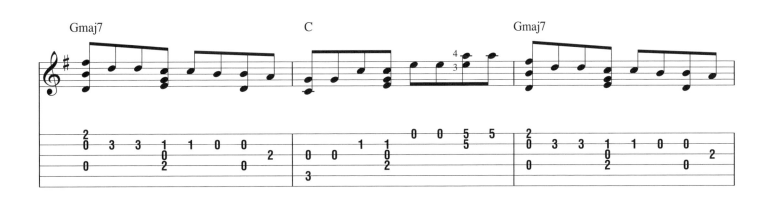

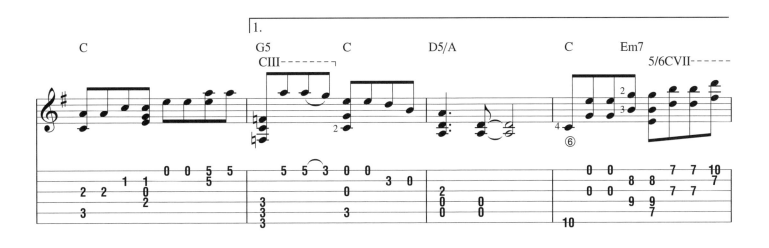

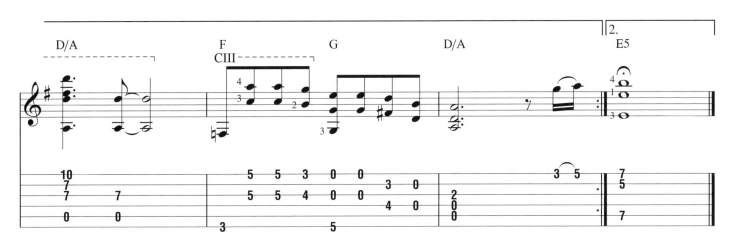

Dreamship

Words and Music by Diana Rae and Patty Way

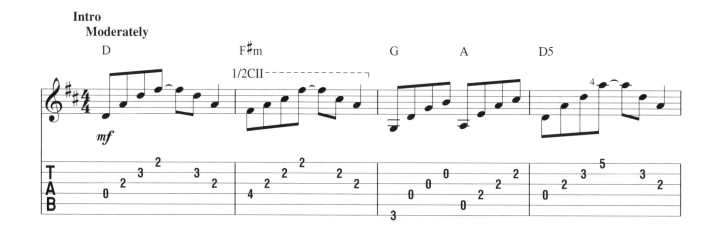

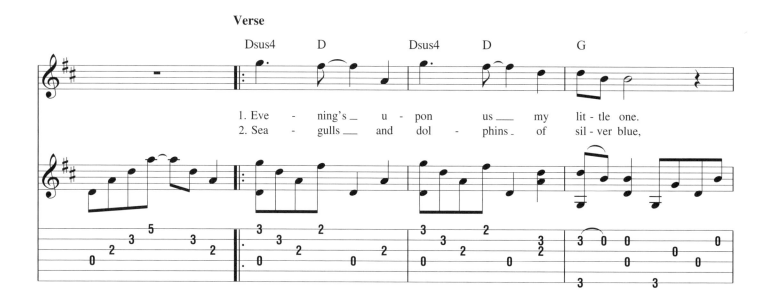

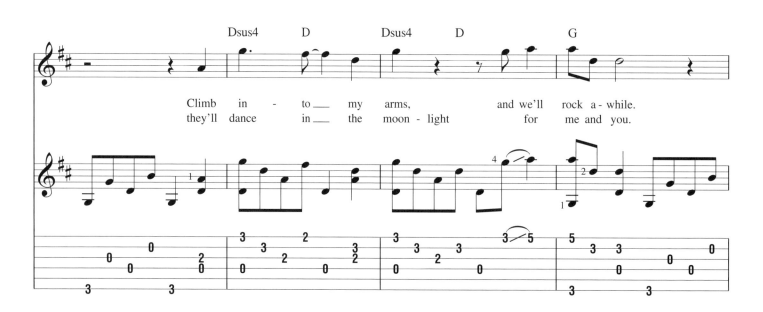

Let me hold you close ___ to me, ___ and
We'll count the stars up in ___ the ___ sky ___ and sing a

we can make ___ be - lieve ___ we're gent - ly rock - ing back ___
sail - or's lul - la - by. ___ So come and rest your sleep -

___ and forth ___ up - on the sea.
- y head ___ and close your eyes. And we'll go

Chorus

sail-ing a - way __ on a dream - ship in - to a star - ry __ night, and the

man in the moon __ will guide __ us with __ his gold - en __ light. __ We'll

raise the sails __ and ride the waves. We've all night long __ to spend.

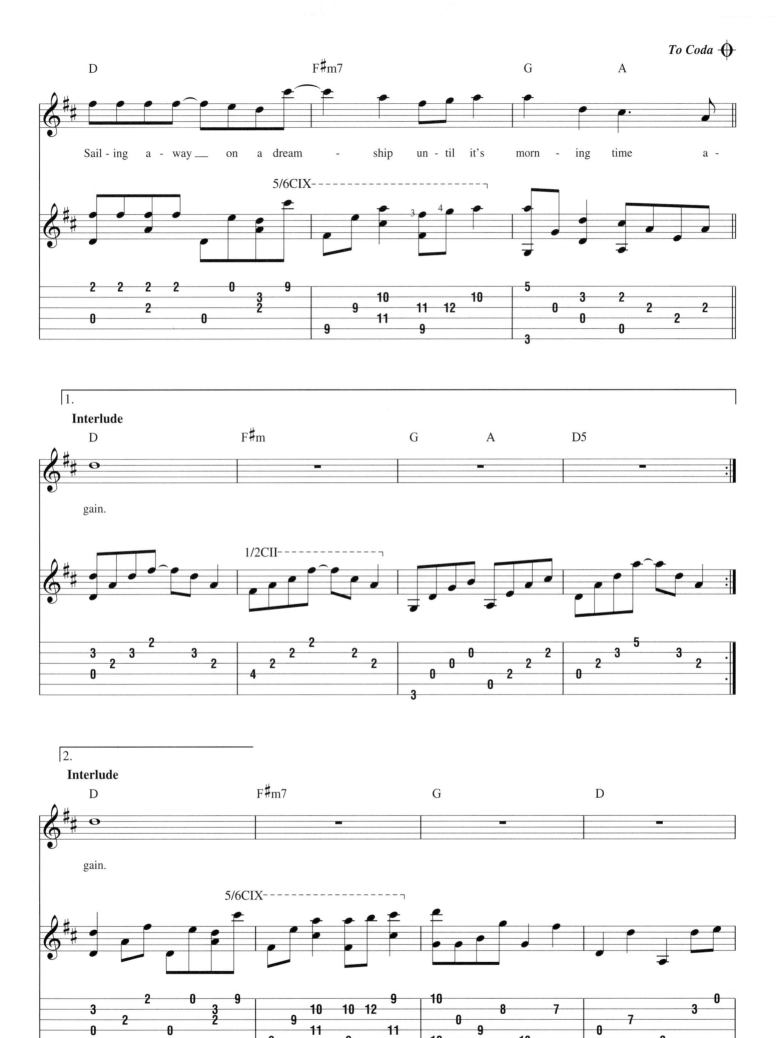

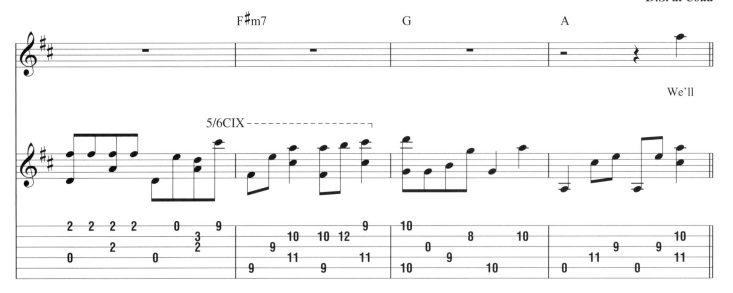

We'll

Coda

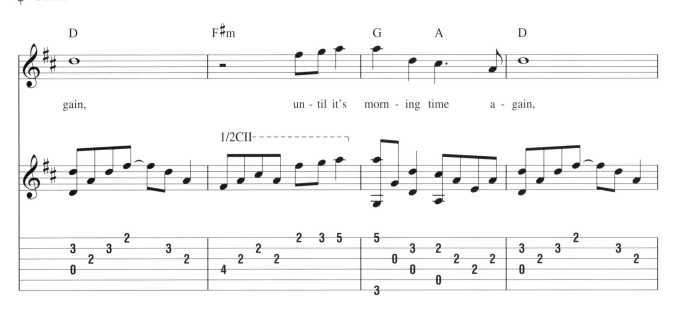

gain, un - til it's morn - ing time a - gain,

un - til it's morn - ing time a - gain.

Good Night

Words and Music by John Lennon and Paul McCartney

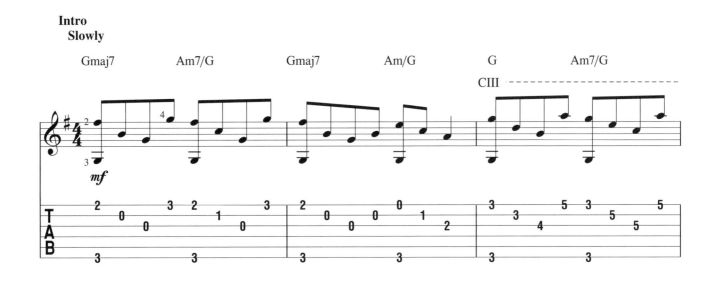

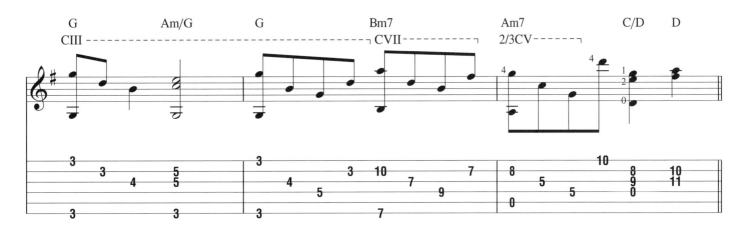

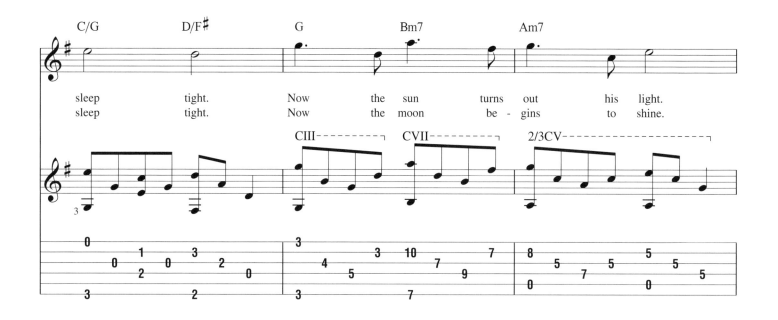

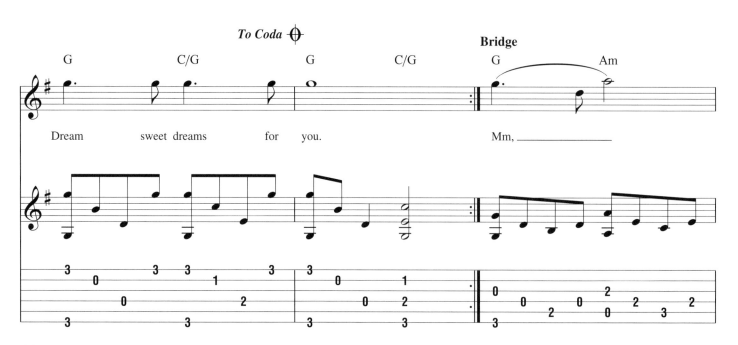

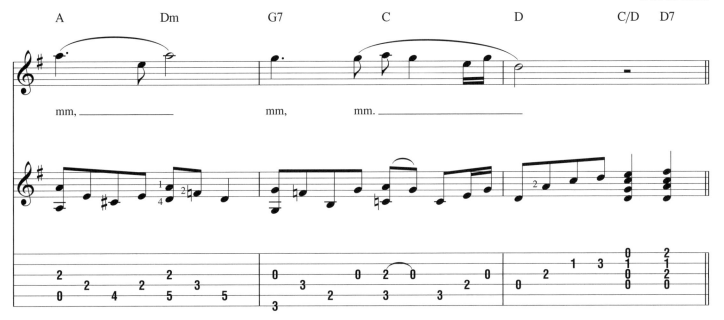

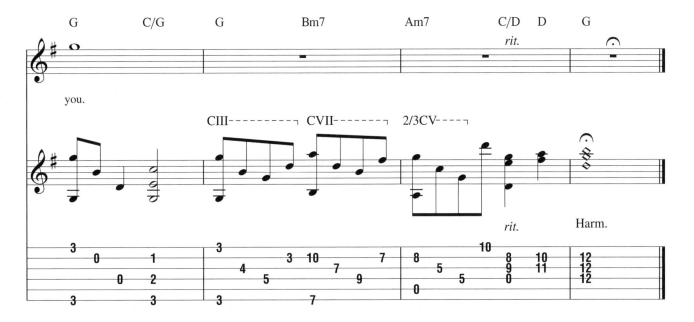

Additional Lyrics

3. Close your eyes, and I'll close mine.
   Good night, sleep tight.
   Now the sun turns out his light.
   Good night, sleep tight.

Hushabye Street

Words and Music by Bonnie Nichols

Intro
Moderately

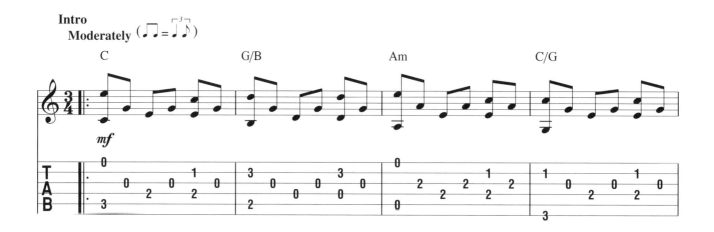

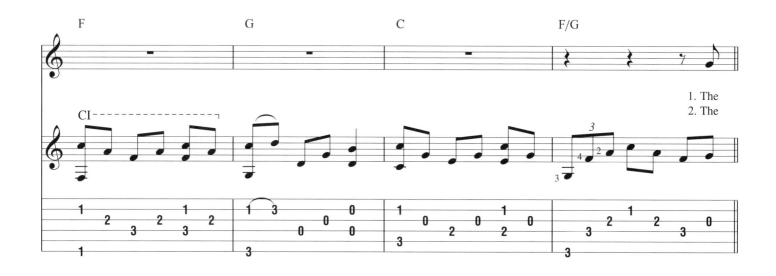

1. The
2. The

Verse

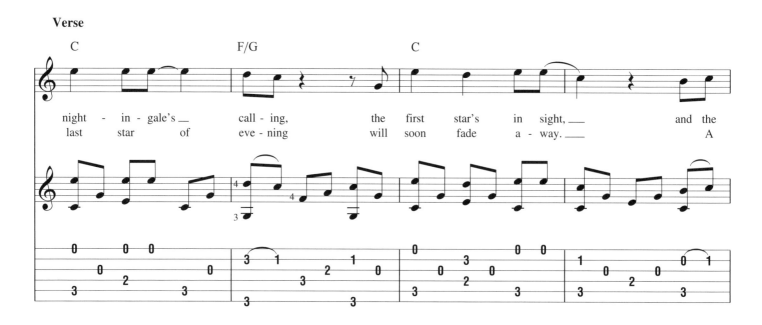

night - in - gale's __ call - ing, the first star's in sight, __ and the

last star of eve - ning will soon fade a - way. __ A

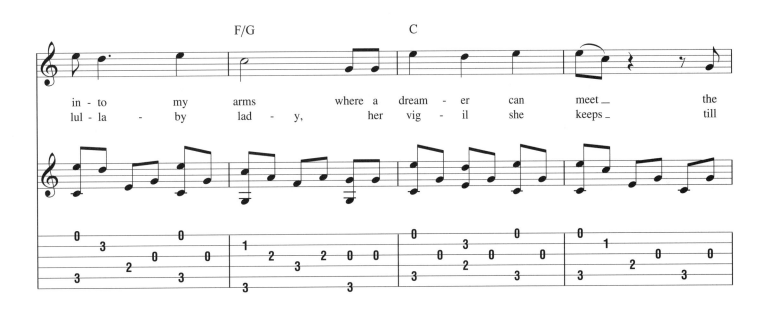

𝄋 Chorus

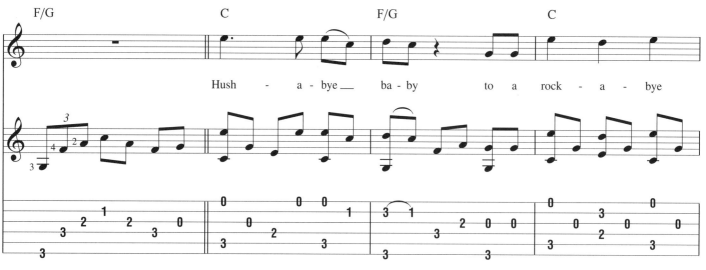

Hush - a - bye __ ba - by to a rock - a - bye

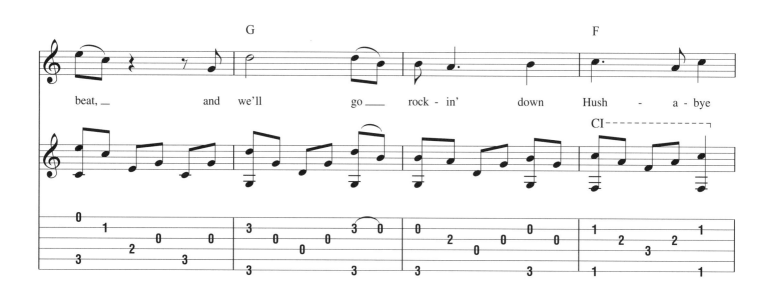

beat, __ and we'll go __ rock - in' down Hush - a - bye

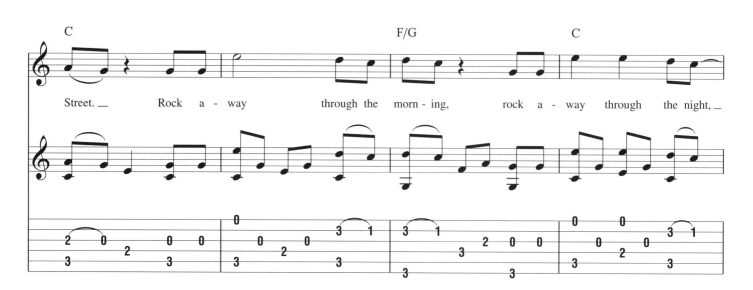

Street. __ Rock a - way through the morn - ing, rock a - way through the night, __

rock a - way   in   the arms _____   that are hold - ing you

1.   **2.**   *D.S. al Coda*   ⊕ **Coda**

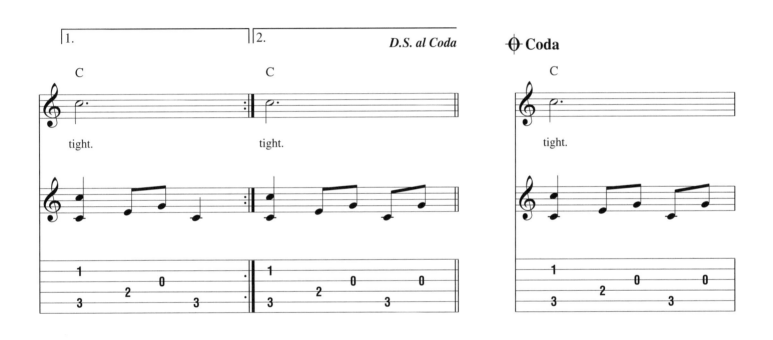

tight.   tight.   tight.

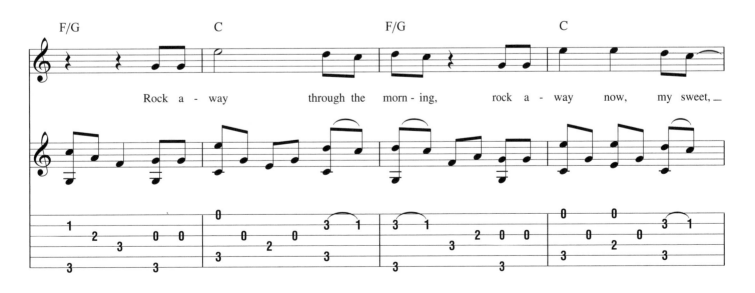

Rock a - way   through the morn - ing,   rock a - way   now,   my sweet, __

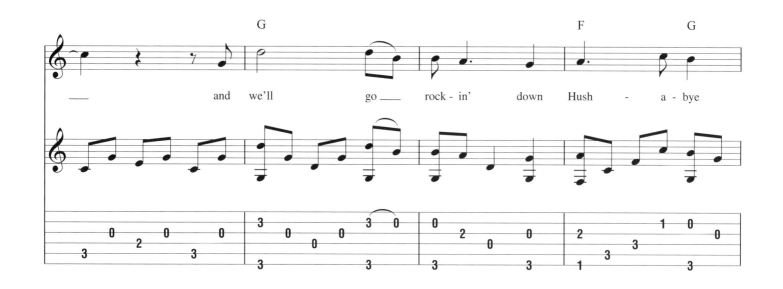

and we'll go ___ rock - in' down Hush - a - bye

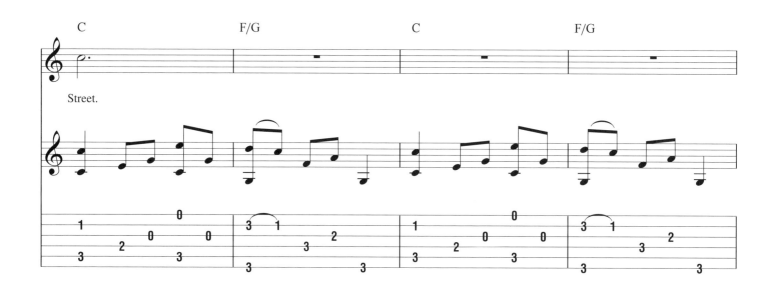

Street.

rit.

I Have a Dream

from MAMA MIA!

Words and Music by Benny Andersson and Björn Ulvaeus

1. I have a

(3.) dream,   a song to sing   to help me
dream,   a fan- tas- y   to help me

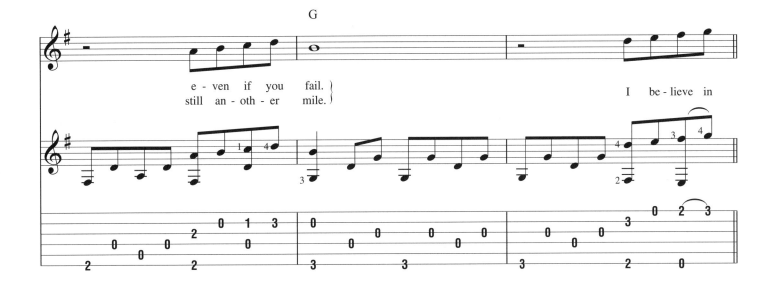

Chorus

time   is   right   for   me,   I'll   cross   the   stream.

I   have   a   dream.   2.I   have   a   I'll   cross   the

Interlude

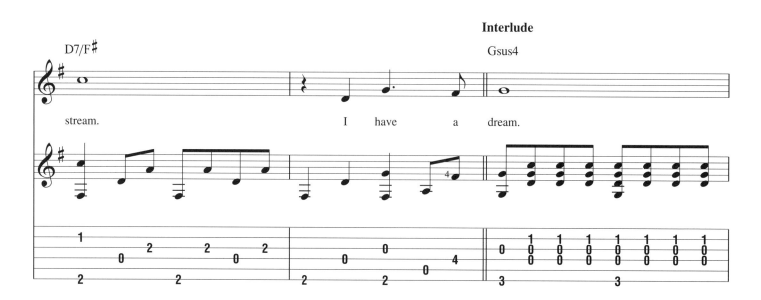

stream.   I   have   a   dream.

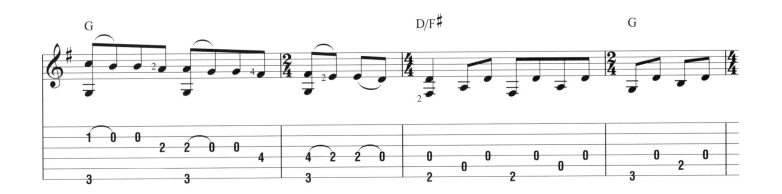

To Coda ⊕

D.S. al Coda
(take 2nd ending)

3. I have a

⊕ **Coda**

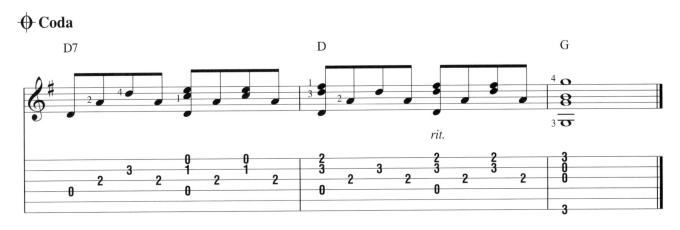

rit.

I L.O.V.E. Y.O.U.

Words and Music by William T. McDuffee and Barry Winslow

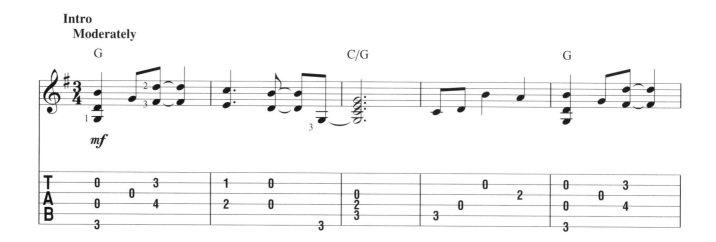

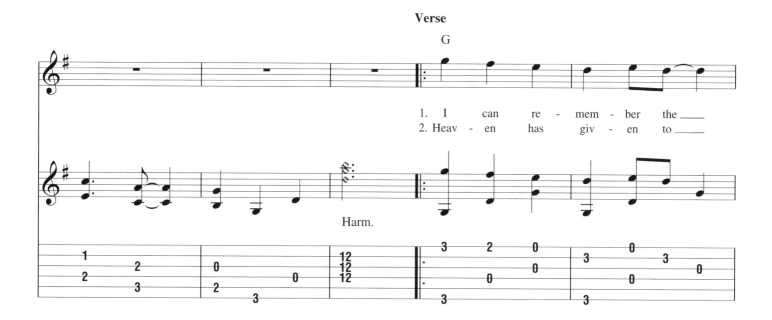

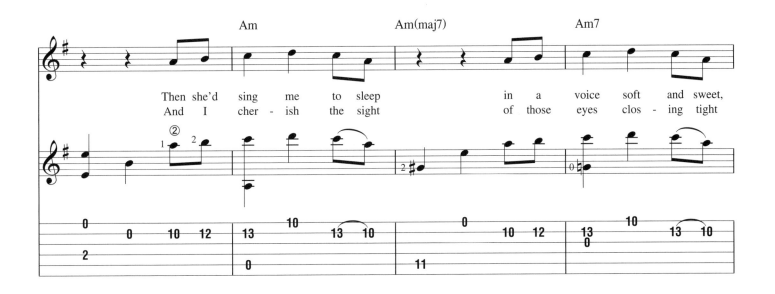

Then she'd sing me to sleep in a voice soft and sweet,
And I cher - ish the sight of those eyes clos - ing tight

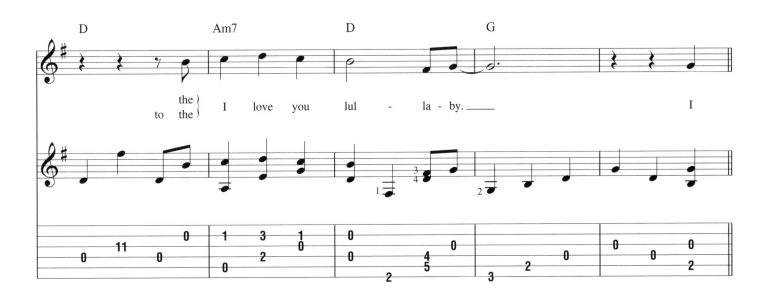

the
to the I love you lul - la - by. ____ I

𝄋 Chorus

L. O. V. E. Y. O. U. You're all of my ____

To Coda ⊕

Interlude

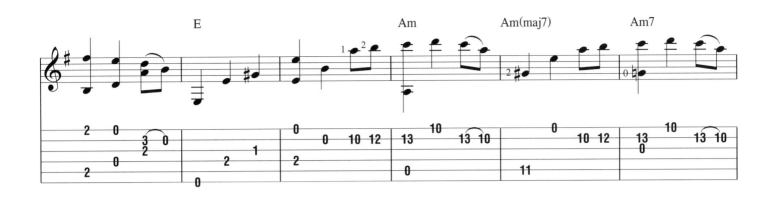

D.S. al Coda

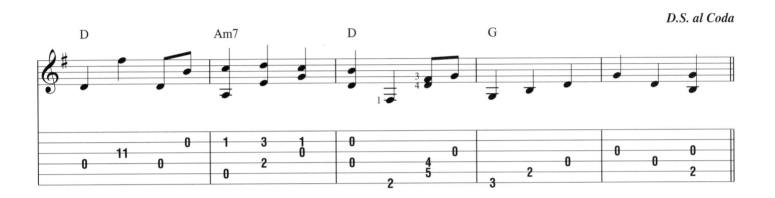

U.   I   L.   O.   V.   E.   Y.   O.   U.

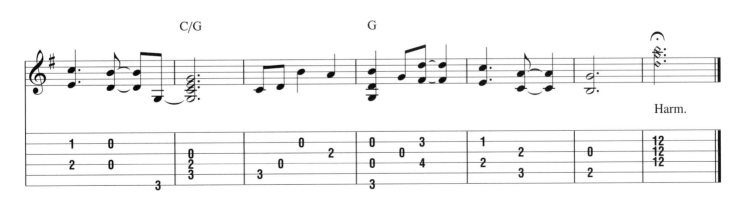

Harm.

I'll Love You Forever

Words and Music by Tedd French and Terry Toler

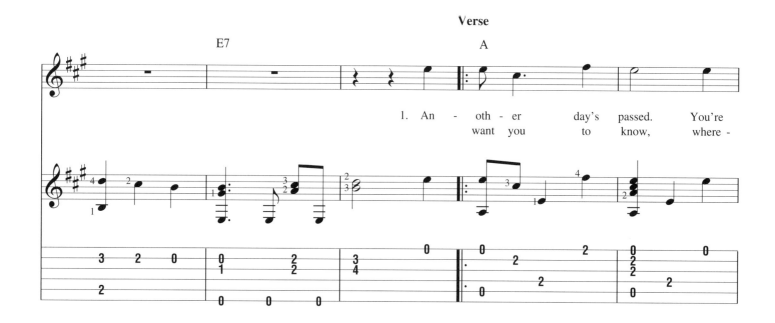

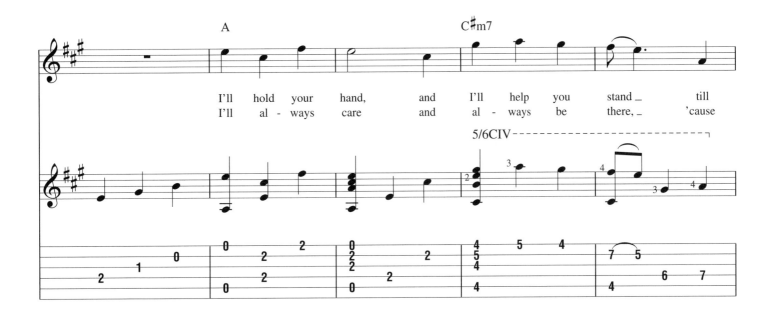

I'll hold your hand, and I'll help you stand _ till
I'll al - ways care and al - ways be there, _ 'cause

Chorus

one day you'll walk on your ___ own.
Ma - ma's _ love lives in the heart. ___

And I'll

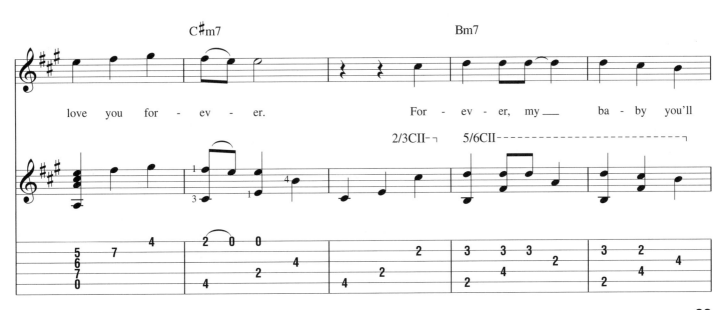

love you for - ev - er.

For - ev - er, my ___ ba - by you'll

Interlude

be.

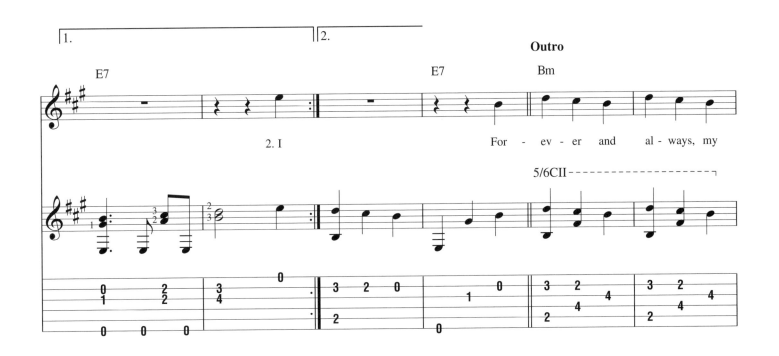

2. I

Outro

For - ev - er and al - ways, my

ba - by you'll be.

I'll Tuck You In

Words and Music by Barbara Bailey Hutchison

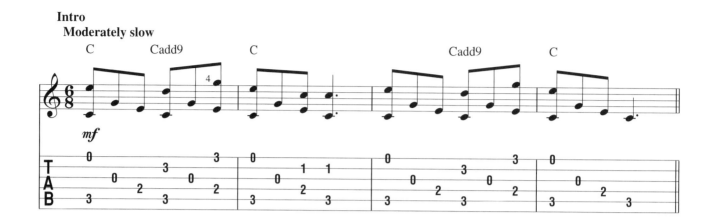

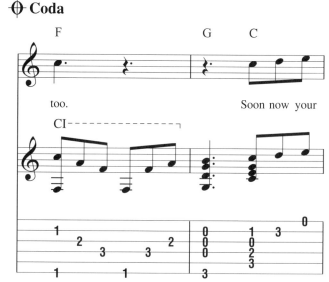

D.S. al Coda

Coda

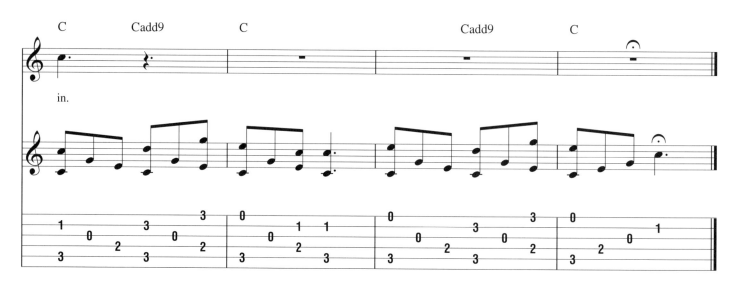

Little Sleepy Eyes

Words and Music by C.C. Couch and Gloria Nissenson

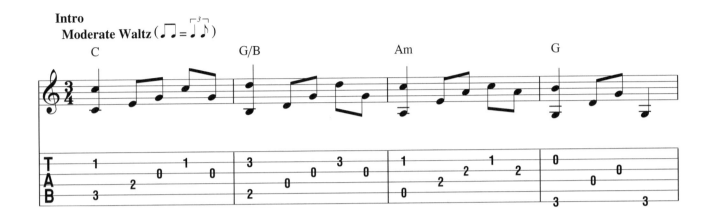

birds are too ___ tired to sing.
sun has put ___ out its light.
Ducks have stopped ___
Mom - my will _____

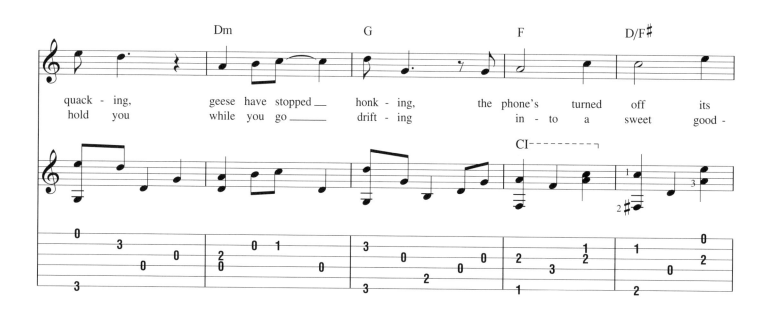

quack - ing, geese have stopped ___ honk - ing, the phone's turned off its
hold you while you go _____ drift - ing in - to a sweet good -

ring. Lambs have stopped ___ baa - ing, dog - gies stopped ___
night. Hush now my lit - tle one, day - time is

bark - ing,   chicks are too ___ tired to peep.
o - ver,   pale moon is ___ up a - bove.

Li - on's stopped ___ roar - ing,   now he's just snor - ing. All the
It would be ___ best now   if you'd just rest now, safe in the

Chorus

world's a - sleep.
arms of love.   It's time for

my   sings   you ——   lul - la - bies, ——

oh,   those   lit - tle

To Coda ⊕
Interlude

sleep - y eyes. ——

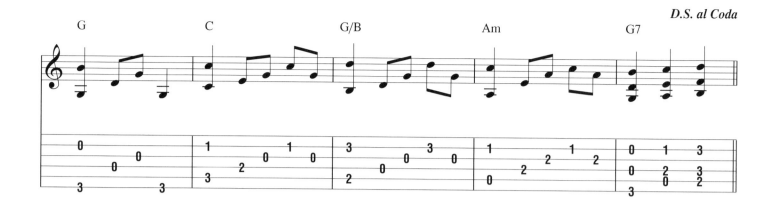

While

mom - my sings you ___ lul - la - bies, ___

Lullaby

Words and Music by Josh Groban, David J. Matthews and Jochem Van Der Saag

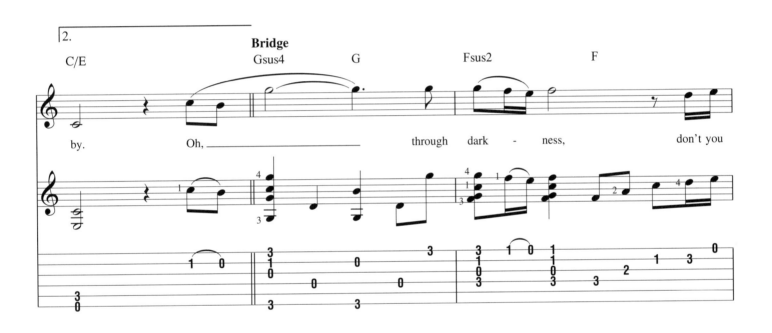

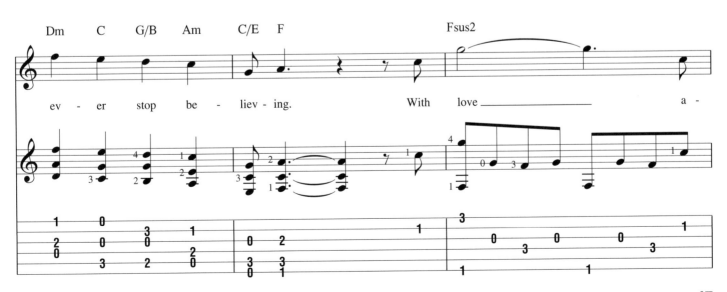

47

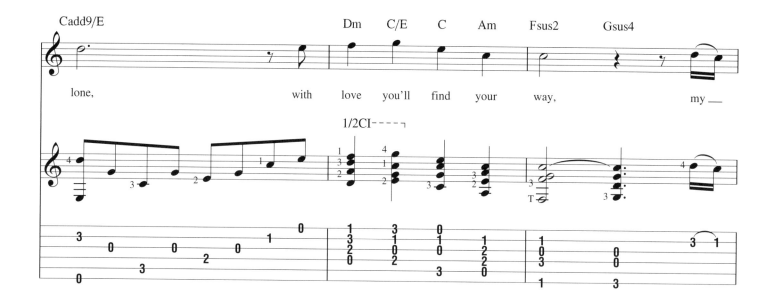

lone, with love you'll find your way, my ___

Verse

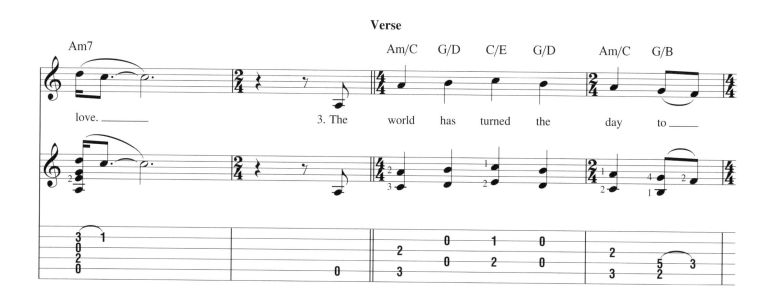

love. _____ 3. The world has turned the day to ___

dark; I leave this __ night with heav - y _____ heart. _ When

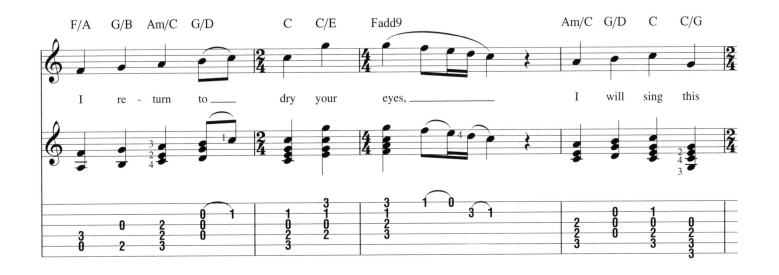

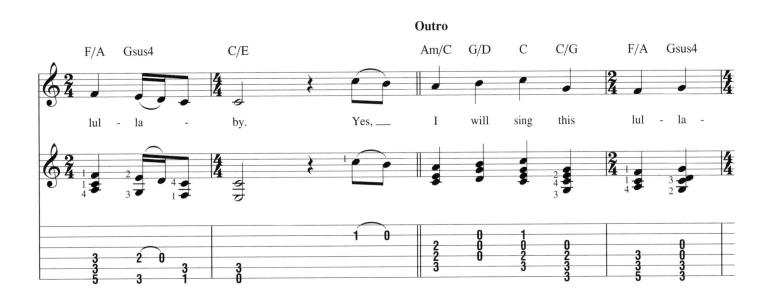

Outro

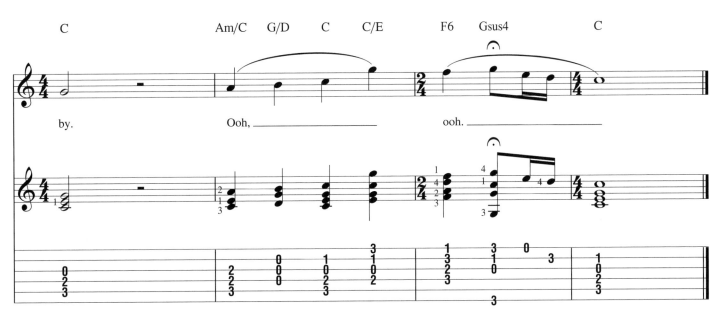

Lullaby for Teddy

Words and Music by Terry Toler

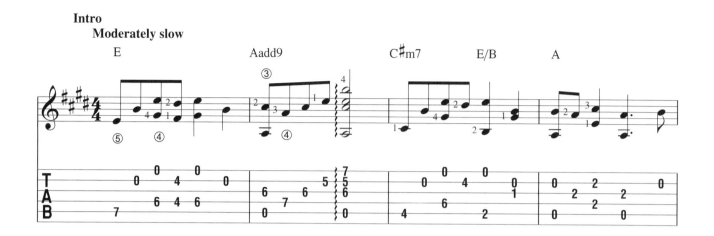

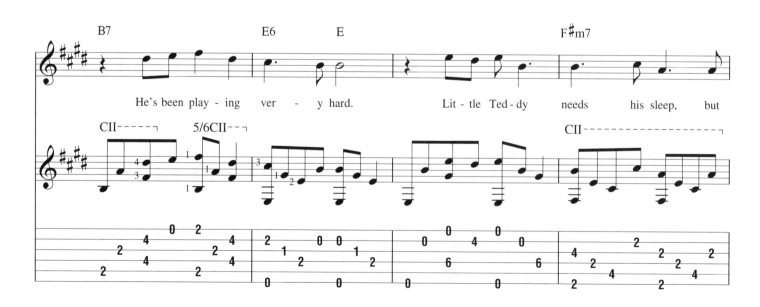

Verse

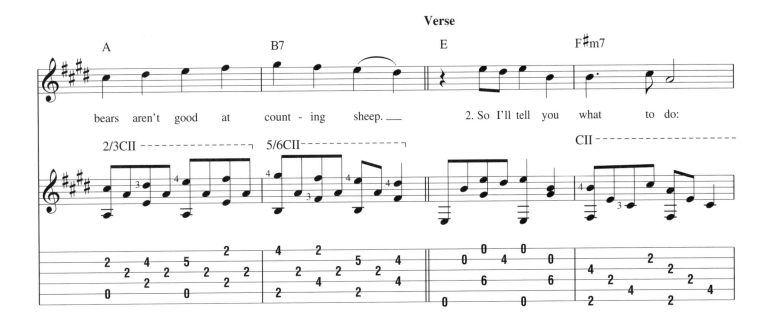

bears aren't good at count - ing sheep. ___ 2. So I'll tell you what to do:

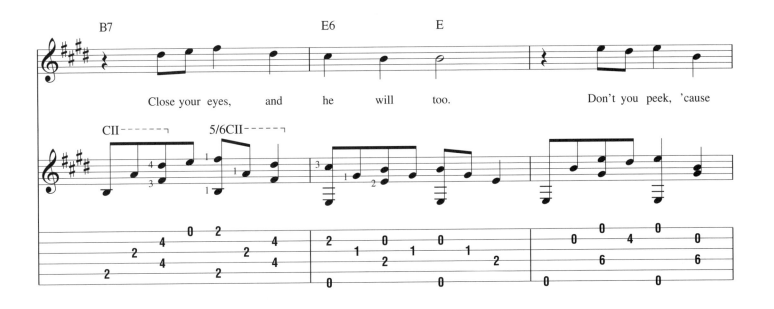

Close your eyes, and he will too. Don't you peek, 'cause

he'll see you. Close your eyes, and he will too. ___

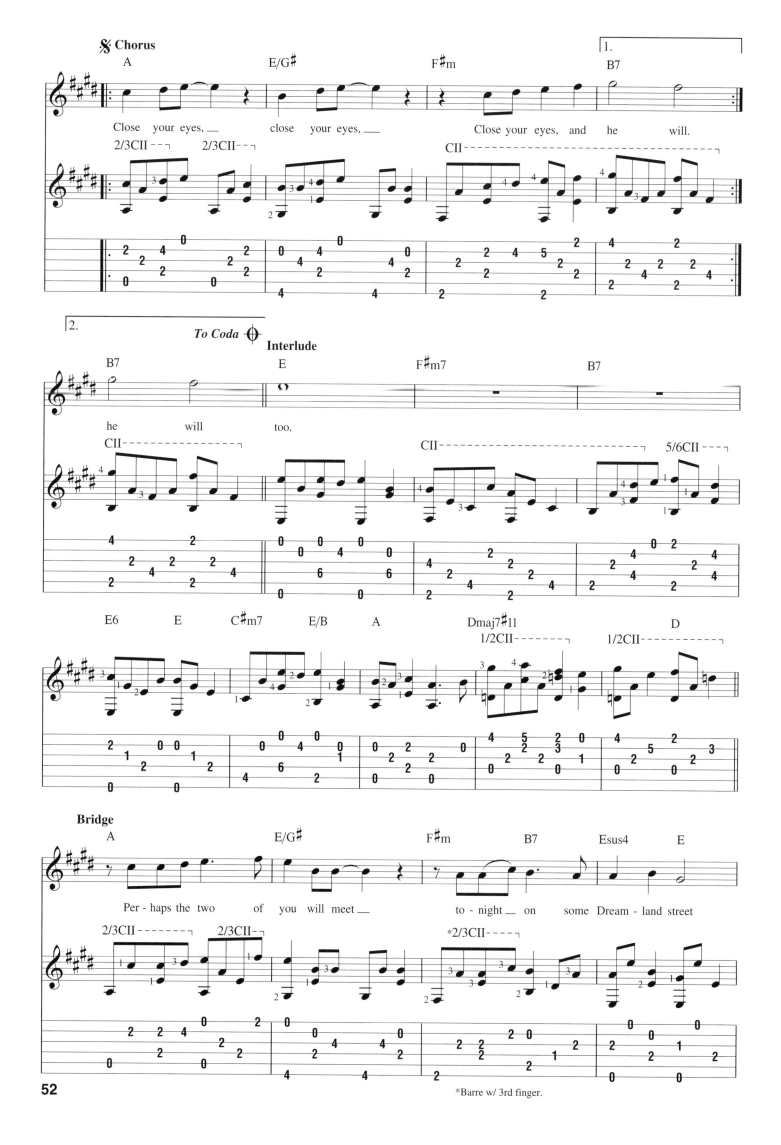

*Barre w/ 3rd finger.

and play to - geth - er through the night, ___ while I sit here __ and hold you tight.

⊕ Coda

too.

Close your eyes, and he will

Outro
A tempo

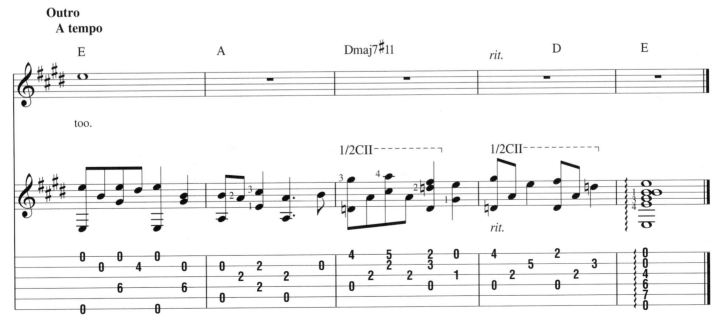

too.

Lullabye (Goodnight, My Angel)

Words and Music by Billy Joel

Intro
Moderately slow

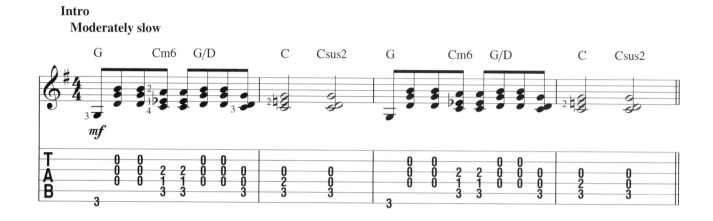

Verse

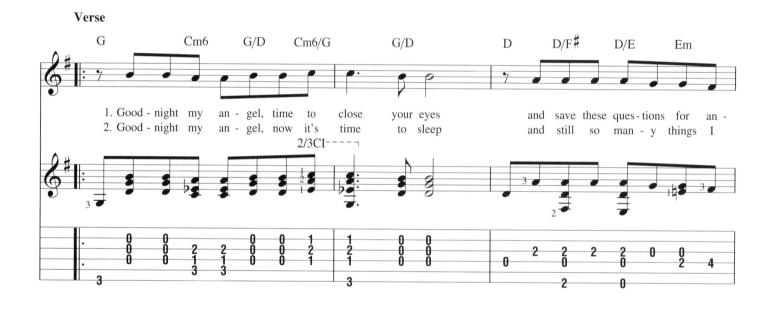

1. Good - night my an - gel, time to close your eyes and save these ques - tions for an -
2. Good - night my an - gel, now it's time to sleep and still so man - y things I

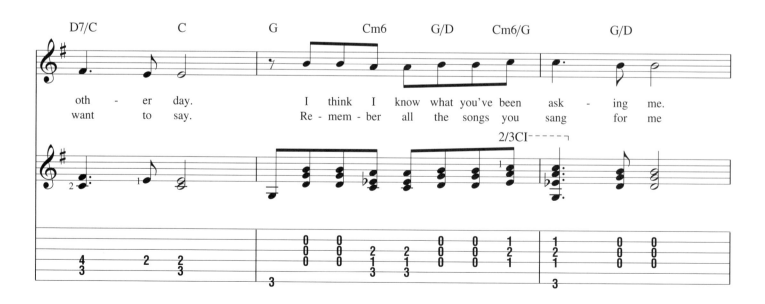

oth - er day. I think I know what you've been ask - ing me.
want to say. Re - mem - ber all the songs you sang for me

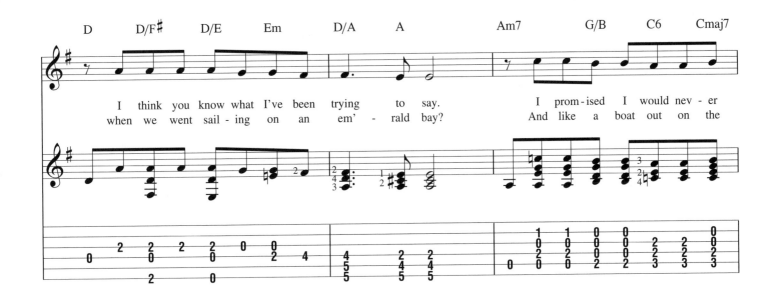

life   will be.   Some-day your child may cry,   and   if   you sing this lul - la - by,

then   in   your   heart   there   will   al - ways   be   a   part   of

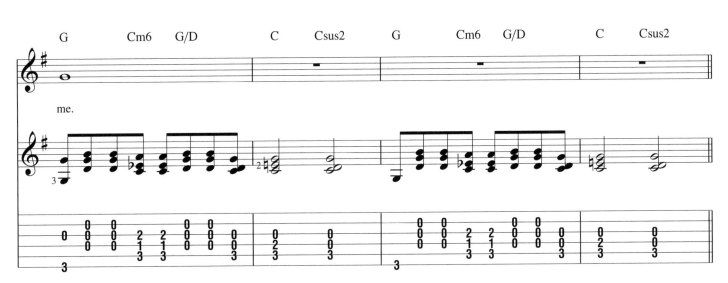

me.

Outro

Some - day we'll all be gone, but lul - la - bies go on and on.

They nev - er die; that's how you and ___ I will

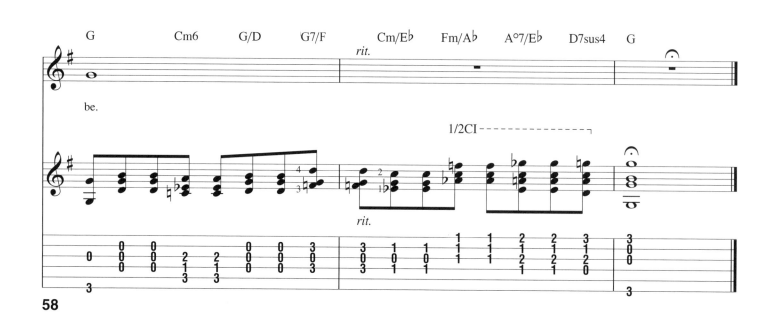

be.

May All Your Dreams Come True

Words and Music by Terry Toler

Intro
Moderate Waltz

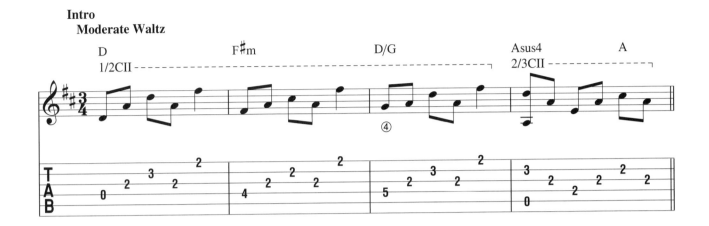

Verse

1. I look ____ at you here in ____ my arms, ____ and
2. Some - day ____ you'll dream of a fam - i - ly,

I know ____ that dreams come true. To -
chil - dren of your own. Per -

night life _____ is sweet, _____ and my dream's _____ com - plete, so I
haps _____ you'll sit in this same rock - ing chair and

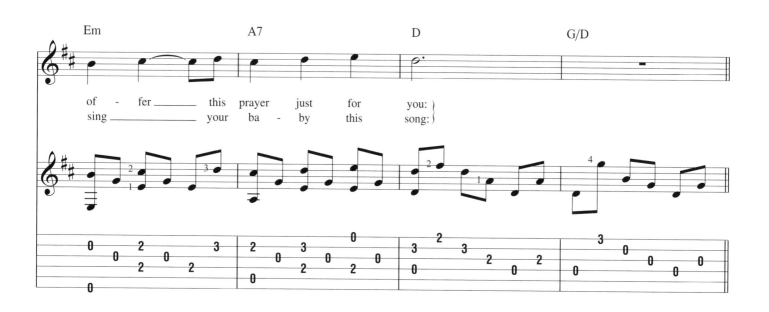

of - fer _____ this prayer just for you: }
sing _____ your ba - by this song: }

Chorus

May all your dreams _____ come true.

May life be good _____ to you.

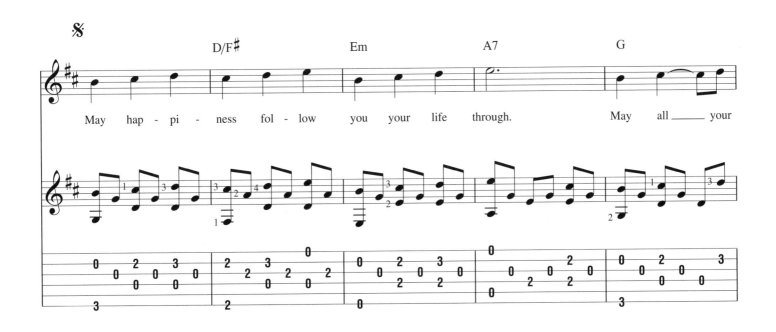

May hap-pi-ness fol-low you your life through. May all ___ your

dreams come __ true.

D.S. al Coda ⊕ **Coda**

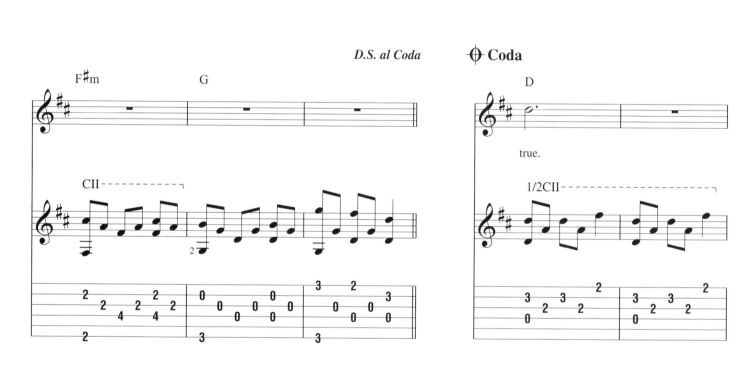

Once Upon a Dream

Words and Music by Susan E. Jacks, Fran Romeo, Lisa Romeo and Lisa Webb

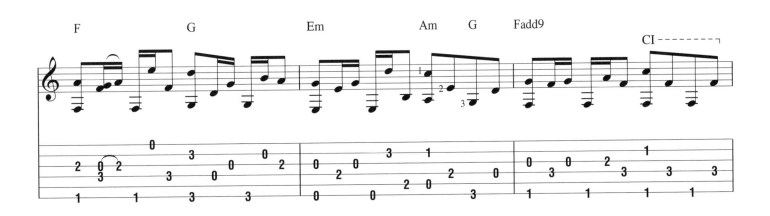

time for us ___ to rest. ___ The moon will keep watch through the night. ___
twin - kle from ___ the eye ___ of a child who's just be - gun to dream. ___

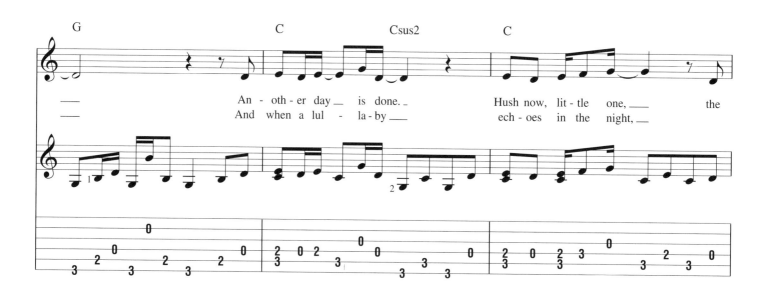

An - oth - er day ___ is done. ___ Hush now, lit - tle one, ___ the
And when a lul - la - by ___ ech - oes in the night, ___

To Coda ⊕

Pre-Chorus

wind is gon - na sing a lul - la - by. And I'll tell you a sto - ry of a
all the stars join in and sing.

ver - y spe - cial place   not so ver - y far __ a - way. __

Chorus

Once up - on __ a dream,   in a sleep-y lit - tle town,   a gen-tle voice __ was heard,   and the

chil - dren gath - ered 'round.   Soft and sweet,   it sang them all __ to sleep.

And a lul - la - by ___ was born   once up - on ___ a dream. ___

Interlude

D.S. al Coda

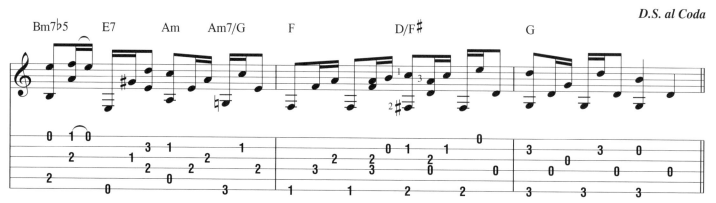

⊕ Coda

Outro-Chorus

Once up-on __ a dream, in a sleep-y lit-tle town, a

gen-tle voice __ was heard, and the chil-dren gath-ered 'round.

Soft and sweet, it sang them all __ to sleep.

Waltzing Down Lullaby Lane

Words and Music by Charles Aaron Wilburn

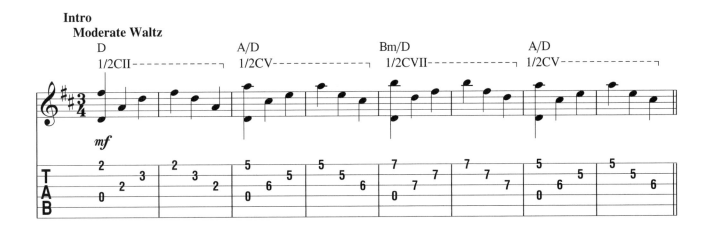

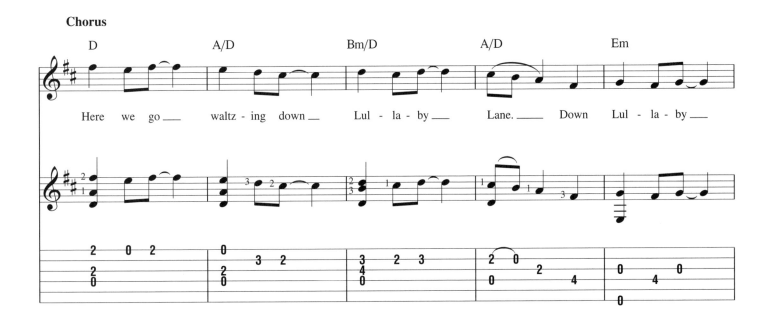

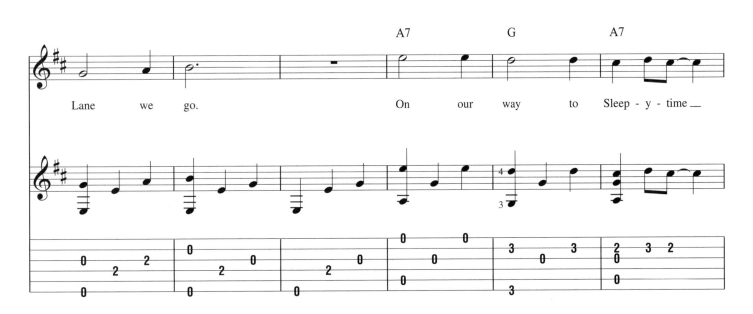

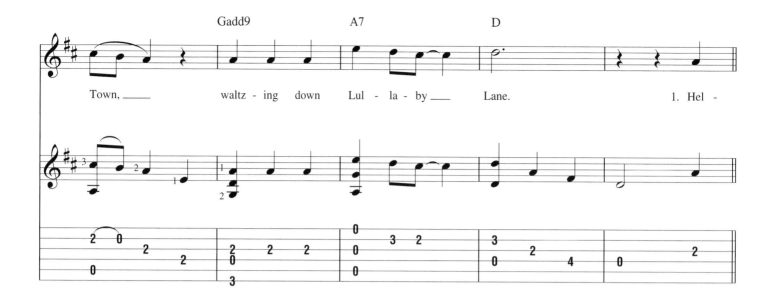

Town,_____ waltz - ing down Lul - la - by ___ Lane. 1. Hel -

𝄋 Verse

lo, Mis - ter Sleep - y, you're here just in time. We're
2. Now Mis - ter Sleep - y is clos - ing his eyes;

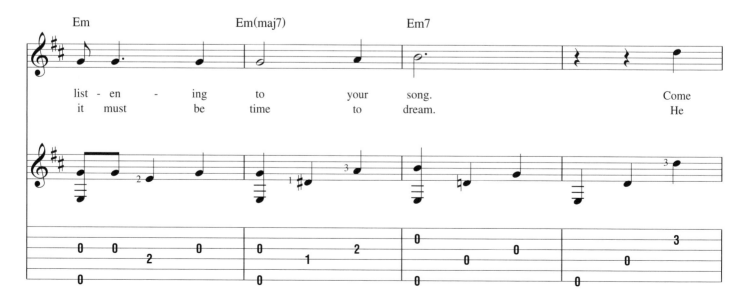

list - en - ing to your song. Come
it must be time to dream. He

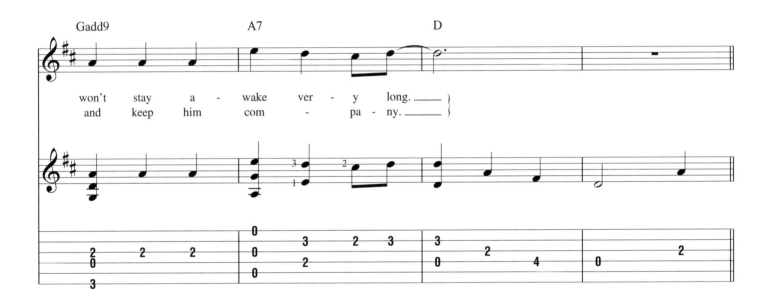

Chorus

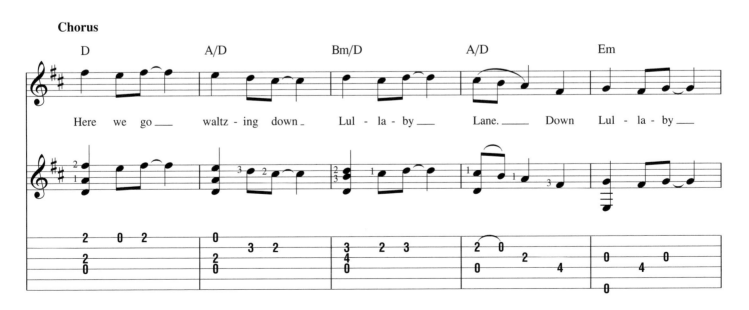